IMAGES
of America

WEST VIRGINIA NATIONAL GUARD 1898–1919

ON THE COVER: Members of Company G, West Virginia National Guard at Marietta, Ohio, are shown in 1912 on their way back from military training at Mount Gretna, Pennsylvania. (Brian S. Kesterson Collection.)

IMAGES
of America

West Virginia National Guard 1898–1919

Brian Stuart Kesterson

ARCADIA
PUBLISHING

ISBN 978-0-7385-6800-3

Published by Arcadia Publishing
Charleston SC, Chicago IL, Portsmouth NH, San Francisco CA

Printed in the United States of America

Library of Congress Control Number: 2009922702

For all general information contact Arcadia Publishing at:
Telephone 843-853-2070
Fax 843-853-0044
E-mail sales@arcadiapublishing.com
For customer service and orders:
Toll-Free 1-888-313-2665

Visit us on the Internet at www.arcadiapublishing.com

This book is dedicated in memory of
Fred M. and Helen Jackson Cochran of Parkersburg,
West Virginia, and to all those who served.

CONTENTS

Acknowledgments

A note of thanks is extended to the following people for their kindness in the publication of this volume: Terry Lowery, Debra Basham, and the staff at the West Virginia Division of Culture and History, Charleston, West Virginia; Kenneth R. Baily, Charleston, West Virginia; Donna Setler, Newport, Ohio; John S. D. Eisenhower, Trappe, Maryland; Anne Elenz, Leesburg, Florida; Bob Mayer, Parkersburg, West Virginia; Luke Cunningham, Arcadia Publishing, Mount Pleasant, South Carolina; Lindsay Harris, Arcadia Publishing, Mount Pleasant, South Carolina; and Mark Pratt, Parkersburg, West Virginia. A special note of thanks is also extended to the following National Park Service rangers: Terrence Winschel, Vicksburg National Military Park; James Ogden, Chickamauga–Chattanooga National Military Park; and Charlie Spearman, Shiloh National Military Park. Unless otherwise noted, all images appear courtesy of the author's collection, including the Fred Cochran collection.

INTRODUCTION

We all have heard the old adage, "One man's trash is another man's treasure." This book is literally based on that premise. In 1997, while on an outing of exploring antique stores in Ohio, I came across this wonderful collection of photographs that had once belonged to Parkersburg, West Virginia, native Fred Cochran. The photographs had been rescued out of a trash can by a man who sold them to an antique dealer in Athens, Ohio. Upon seeing the photographs, I set out to purchase the entire collection, which at first posed a bit of a problem as the dealer wanted to sell them all separately. A deal was eventually worked out. The dealer traded for my 1850 officer's sword, 200 Native American arrowheads, and my prized Hopewell-Adena pole celt—a sacrifice that I didn't really want to make, but the extreme rarity of West Virginia National Guard photographs from 1913 to 1918 even surpasses those scarce Civil War photographs, which collectors gobble up at a drop of a hat. There was only one picture that he would not part with, and that was of an early, military, converted Harley-Davidson motorcycle. With my main objective of saving nearly the entire collection now accomplished, I set out on a series of fact-finding missions. Unfortunately to my disappointment, I discovered that the guard reports for this time period were lost or destroyed many years ago. Surviving guard material for this time period is now housed at the West Virginia Division of Culture and History in Charleston, West Virginia.

My research eventually led me to a book published by Kenneth R. Baily titled *Mountaineers Are Free: A History of the West Virginia National Guard*. This book was of great help to me in understanding the formation and organization of the guard. The book also helped me fill in important information directly dealing with these photographs. A special note of thanks is extended to Baily for his interest in this project. A special note of thanks is also extended to John S. D. Eisenhower of Trappe, Maryland, for his verification on several of the photographs that appeared staged.

The Cochran collection is by far the best collection of grouped photographs from this time period, but they are not the only photographs of the guard from this time period. The C. V. Feller Collection, housed at the West Virginia Division of Culture and History in Charleston, also gives a good view of the guard. The center also has an interesting collection of guard photographs from the West Virginia Mine Wars era. Some of these photographs appear in this publication as well. A special note of thanks goes to Debra Basham at the West Virginia Division of Culture and History for getting me copies of several of the photographs that are used in this publication. A special note of thanks is also extended to Terry Lowery of the West Virginia Division of Culture and History for his assistance in this publication.

With any luck, more photographs of the guard may turn up after the publication of this book. It is my hope that people will realize how valuable these types of images are to future generations and historians. It is important that we share our history with others. If we as a people can't draw on our past and learn the lessons that came from it, then how can we expect future generations to view us and preserve the past if we did not take the time to do it ourselves?

One could say that the formation of a guard-like unit in western Virginia was based on the old Virginia Militia system. The first organized militia company in what is now present-day West Virginia was first founded by Morgan Morgan, who had been commissioned as a captain in the Virginia Militia on February 17, 1735. Under his watchful eye and supervision, the Berkely Riflemen had been formed to help protect white settlers from hostile Native American raids on the Virginia frontier.

The militia system proved to be an important asset to the early (West) Virginians who continued to build and expand on their frontier. As each new region was settled, and with the development of each new county, so developed a new local militia unit for each. These units would eventually become the nucleus of the fine fighting forces that would later serve in the French and Indian War, the Revolutionary War, the War of 1812, the Mexican-American War, and the Civil War. Western Virginian militiamen took part in every major campaign or battle in our nation's history from 1754 to 1865. It was from this very militia system that the birth and growth of the West Virginia National Guard came into being in 1889.

From the years 1865 to 1889, the West Virginia militia waxed and waned as recruitment dropped. With funding being at a bare minimum on the state and local levels, some units nearly ceased to exist. Some unit officers were even reduced to paying out of their own pockets to keep their organizations in the field. On the state and local levels, it became apparent that nearly all interest in having a state militia was put on the back burner. The state had continually called upon and depended on the militia to settle labor and strike disputes in the coalfields, but very little, if any, help was extended to the militia from the powers that held the purse strings.

In 1889, new legislation was passed by the congress, which provided badly needed funding for state military organizations. Under this new legislation, the guard was placed on a more equal footing with the regular army. This act standardized weapons, uniforms, and military drill to match that of the regular U.S. Army. Today the members of the modern West Virginia National Guard can look back and be proud of the roots from which they sprang. This book is as much for their sakes as it is to document the lives of the West Virginia National Guardsmen who came before them.

Respectfully,
Brian Stuart Kesterson
Lubeck, West Virginia

One

Formation of the Guard

From Militiamen to Guardsmen

This photograph is identified as, "J. W. Batkin, Company K, First West Virginia Volunteer Infantry at Camp Poland, Knoxville, Tennessee." An officer wears the Model 1895 undress blouse. Another wears the 1874 officer's pattern belt plate and the 1880-pattern summer helmet. Many enlisted men are wearing the five-button 1874-pattern blouse. Others wear the 1883-pattern blue shirt. Some men exhibit the 1872-pattern U.S. belt plate. In 1889, Congress passed new legislation standardizing weapons, uniforms, and military drill to match the regular U.S. Army. With the outbreak of the Spanish-American War, the 2nd West Virginia Regiment was made active on July 9, 1898. Around August 1st, the regiment was ordered to Camp Mead near Harrisburg, Pennsylvania, for drill and maneuvers. On November 6th, the regiment was ordered to Greenville, South Carolina, in order to mobilize for action in Cuba. The war ended before the troops were sent. The regiment was mustered out of the service on April 10, 1899. The guard took no active part in the Spanish-American War but was held stateside in Pennsylvania, Georgia, and South Carolina.

This Spanish-American War–era photograph features three enlisted men of Company L, 1st West Virginia Volunteer Infantry (West Virginia National Guard) standing in front of the mess area. The men are wearing what appears to be the Spanish-American War, Mills pattern 45/70 Krag cartridge belt with the U.S. Mills pattern belt plate. All three of these men are wearing the five button 1874-pattern blouse. They are also holding bayonets in their hands. The guns stacked in the foreground are believed to be the M1896 configuration Krag-Jorgensen rifle. The original copy of this photograph is heavily water damaged and the location where this photograph was taken has been lost.

Two

Mother Jones and the West Virginia National Guard

Mary Harris "Mother" Jones, also known as "The Miner's Angel," first made her appearance in the West Virginia coal fields in December 1900. She proved to be a stalwart and outspoken advocate for human rights. In speaking of West Virginia, she stated, "Why, the Czar of Russia, tyrant that he is, is a gentleman compared with some of the fellows there who oppress these people. I AM GOING BACK THERE!" (West Virginia State Archives, West Virginia Coal Life Collection.)

In July 1912, the guard attended the joint U.S. Army maneuvers at Mount Gretna, Pennsylvania, but because of the strike situation, which had flared up again in the coalfields along Paint Creek, Gov. William Glasscock decided to recall the guardsmen and directed the men to return to the state for duty on Paint Creek. By August, the guardsmen were able to attend their joint exercises in Pennsylvania. Fred Cochran is pictured above.

This member of Company G, 2nd West Virginia National Guard, is only identified with the name "Ora." This photograph was taken outside of the Ohio National Guard Armory while the men in the 2nd West Virginia National Guard were laying over at Marietta, Ohio, after coming back from joint military maneuvers at Mount Gretna, Pennsylvania. While at Marietta, the men took some time to sightsee and visit friends in the "Pioneer City." After a brief rest, the men of the 2nd West Virginia National Guard were on their way back to the troubled coalfields of West Virginia. Today the Ohio National Guard Armory has been placed on the National Register of Historic Places. When the century-old structure was threatened with demolition in 2006, concerned citizens stepped forward to save the site, thus preserving part of Ohio's National Guard heritage.

STANDARD W. VA. AUG 12 A.M. 1912

THIS SIDE OF CARD IS FOR ADDRESS ONLY

Miss Sina Morehead
united Woolen Mills
Parkersburg
W Va

This postcard from Osie Morehead, of Company E, 2nd West Virginia National Guard, is dated August 12, 1912. Morehead, in writing to his mother and sister in Parkersburg, West Virginia, assures them that he and his fellow guardsmen are all doing well after armed miners at Standard, West Virginia, fired upon the camp the previous night. Such nighttime sniping and small skirmishes were not uncommon for this time period in West Virginia National Guard history. The mining camps along Paint and Cabin Creeks were a virtual powder keg with a short fuse, ready to go off without a moment's notice. Diplomacy, fair play, and compassion for the plight of the miners helped ease tensions between the miners and the guardsmen in the camps, but the situation was a cautious one to say the least.

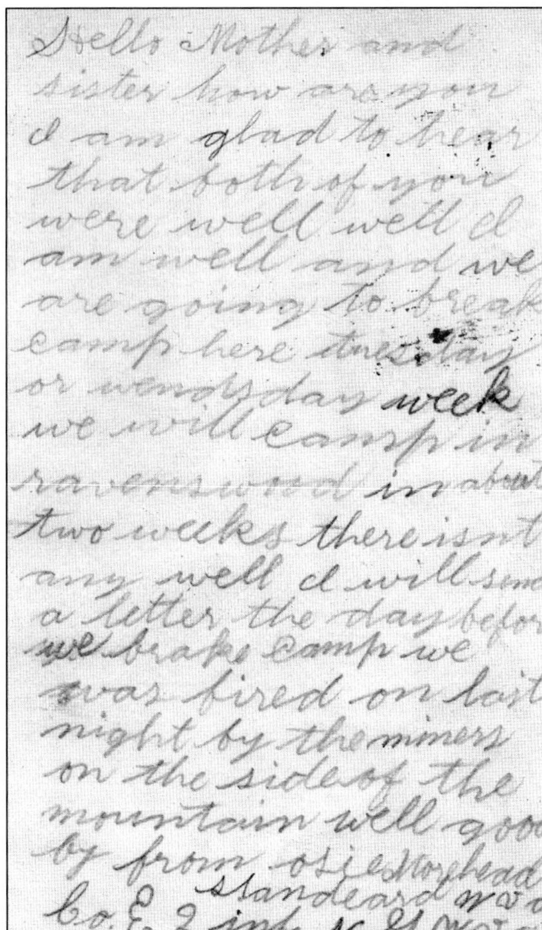
Hello Mother and
sister how are you
I am glad to hear
that both of you
were well well I
am well and we
are going to break
camp here tuesday
or wendsday week
we will camp in
ravenswood in about
two weeks there isnt
any well I will send
a letter the day before
we brake camp we
was fired on last
night by the miners
on the side of the
mountain well good
by from osie Morehead
standeard W Va
Co. E 2 inf N.G. W Va

Members of Company G, 2nd West Virginia National Guard, are pictured at Marietta, Ohio, on August 22, 1912, after attending joint maneuvers at Mount Gretna, Pennsylvania. This postcard, even though brief, gives insight that trouble between the miners and mine operators and their hired thugs from the Baldwin-Felts Detective Agency was still brewing on Paint Creek and along other coal camps along the creeks. During the month of August 1912, the soldiers were put to work cleaning up the coal camps, improving the sanitation system, draining swampy areas, and instructing the miners on how to improve their living conditions. Observations made by the officers led them to criticize the mine owners and operators for their lack of effort to keep the camps clean and healthful for the miners. Many National Guardsmen expressed that they believed the miners were being held in a state of peonage or industrial servitude, with the mine guards committing all manner of atrocities upon them.

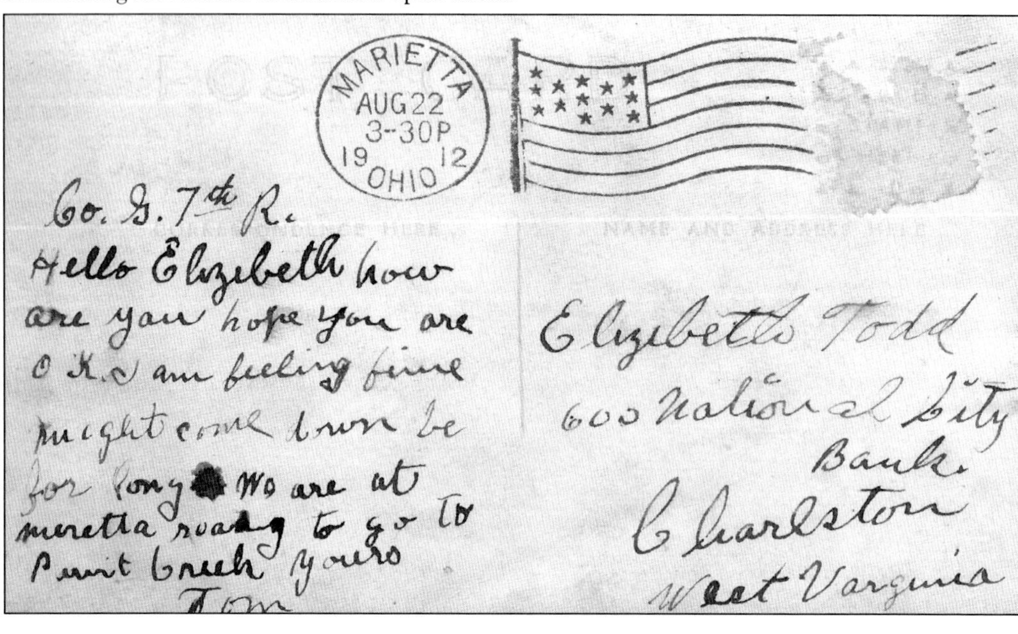

These two photographs of Camp Eskdale show the large encampment of West Virginia National Guard tents in the center of the photograph. The men of the unit went so far as to whitewash rocks and arrange them on the side of the mountain to spell out "CAMP ESKDALE." On August 6, 1912, Mother Jones spoke to a group of miners at Eskdale, located on Cabin Creek. In her typical forceful and rich vocabulary, she expressed to the miners that it was time for them to throw off their chains and organize and only then strike. Shortly after this spirited speech, the strike was on. This photograph was taken shortly after the strike. Guardsmen were sent in to restore order and begin the process of cleaning up the mine camps, promoting better living conditions for the miners and their families.

Lt. Fred Cochran (right) and another officer of the 2nd West Virginia National Guard stand in front of their tent at Standard, West Virginia. Both the 1st and 2nd Regiments were stationed at Standard during the 1912 strikes. Conditions on Paint Creek improved when Governor Glasscock proposed an investigation into the claims and counterclaims of the miners and operators. As the commission prepared for its investigation, the governor relieved five companies, leaving four on duty in the strike zone. On August 30, a pitched battle broke out between miners on Cabin Creek and mine guards at Dry Branch. The result of this skirmish left one mine guard dead. Governor Glasscock ordered Companies A, F, G, H, and an additional company from the provisional headquarters to mobilize from their home bases and to report to Cabin Creek and restore order.

Members of the 2nd Regiment are pictured in an open order drill at Camp Eskdale in 1912.

Two photographs show guardsmen drilling and preparing for inspection at Standard. The guardsmen in previous difficulties had managed to keep a friendly disposition between themselves and the miners. Now the situation between the two groups was starting to deteriorate. The miners started demanding that the guardsmen along the creeks and guarding the trains be removed. The guardsmen received orders to prevent any type of public gatherings from taking place, an order they were ever vigilant to uphold. The order also included gatherings that featured union organizers such as Mary "Mother" Jones. From August 31 to September 2, the miners continued their attacks on the mine guards, and by September 2, a climax was reached, with the miners destroying various sections of the C&O Railroad tracks to keep the trains from taking coal from the mines to market.

Officers of the 2nd West Virginia National Guard relax in their camp at Standard, West Virginia. While the 1st and 2nd West Virginia National Guard were fulfilling their duties, Governor Glasscock issued a proclamation of martial law after evidence of lawlessness. He hoped the guardsmen, along with military courts, could restore order where civilian authorities had failed. Glasscock ordered adjutant general C. D. Elliot to establish a military commission that would be used for trying civilians accused of violations of rules and regulations within the martial law zone. Glasscock also directed Adjutant Elliot to confiscate all arms and ammunition in the area covered by martial law.

While at Camp Standard, the men of the 1st and 2nd West Virginia National Guard did duty along Paint and Cabin Creeks. The 1912 time period proved to be turbulent with strikes, protests, and outright gunplay between the miners and the mine owners' hired mine guards. West Virginia governor William Glasscock repeatedly called upon the guard to settle the tensions in 1912. By September, repeated attacks, destruction of property, and pitched battles between the miners and the mine guards resulted in martial law being declared in the coal camps. The situation did not improve until Dr. Henry Hatfield was elected governor of West Virginia on March 4, 1913.

In the first full day of martial law, the guard confiscated approximately 1,500 rifles, 6 or 7 Colt machine guns, more than 200,000 rounds of ammunition, and literally bushels of pistols. Not all of the arms were collected because of the fact many miners hid their weapons or disappeared into the rugged countryside out of reach of the troops. The weapons that had been confiscated ranged from the very newest Colt machine gun to old Civil War–era muskets and carbines. Martial law helped to improve relations between the miners and the guard, as the guard showed no partiality to either side, but this new feeling of security would be short-lived. The military commission began to try miners and mine guards alike for a variety of offenses ranging from carrying a gun without a license to adultery. During its six weeks of operation, the commission tried, convicted, and sentenced more than 100 people to jail terms. Some of those were remanded to the state prison at Moundsville. (West Virginia State Archives, West Virginia Coal Life Collection, Gravely-Moore Collection.)

Three

The Great Negotiator

On March 4, 1913, Henry Hatfield inherited the Glasscock administration's failed policies. Hatfield had been a physician before becoming governor. Hatfield dressed in his medical corpsman uniform and headed for the coalfields. Hatfield reports, "I noticed a soldier marching to and fro in front of the little cabin on the banks of the Kanawha River. I told the soldier who I was and inquired what responsibility he had there. He told me Mother Jones was being guarded in this little shack and when I entered I found her lying on a straw tick on the floor, carrying a temperature of 104, a very rapid respiration and a constant cough. She had pneumonia. I flagged the first train and had a soldier take her to Charleston where she was placed under the care of a competent physician." Hatfield's repeated trips of mercy to the coalfields brought goodwill and trust among the miners. This new governor was a man of courage, honesty, compassion, and decency. Hatfield ended the strike with his "Hatfield Contract," signed by both parties on May 1, 1913. (West Virginia State Archives.)

In 1913, the Ohio River overflowed its banks and caused untold damage to many cities and towns along the river. This rare postcard photograph of Camp Baker shows the relief shelters and tents that were set up at Ravenswood, West Virginia, to help care for the sick and those displaced by the flood. Soldiers, nurses, and doctors can be seen going about their duties.

In 1914, members of the 2nd West Virginia National Guard went to Camp Dawson near Dunkard Bottom in Preston County, West Virginia, for military maneuvers. In this photograph, the men are at ease while officers on foot and horseback confer to determine the next exercise in the school of the soldier. Camp Dawson was named after West Virginia's 12th governor, William Mercer Owens Dawson, who served from 1905 to 1909.

This photograph of Company E, 2nd West Virginia National Guard, was taken in 1914 while the men and officers were drilling at Camp Dawson. Company E was stationed at Parkersburg, and many of the men in the company came from Wood County and the surrounding counties. Besides a short period of inactivity after World War I, Camp Dawson has been in active operation since 1909.

This rare early scene of Camp Dawson, West Virginia, was taken in 1914. The 1914 campaign season saw Company E, 2nd West Virginia National Guard, doing training maneuvers at the camp and along the Cheat River. The area is known for a varied terrain and climate, and because of this fact, multiple branches of the modern military use the reserve for training today.

As witnessed by these two photographs, a portion of the West Virginia National Guard went on joint military maneuvers with other guard units from across the country at Jacksonville, Florida, in October 1915. These particular cards, dated October 20, 1915, were sent to Lt. Fred Cochran by his friend and fellow officer Lt. Howard E. DeVaughn. DeVaughn jokingly signed the postcard, "Be home Monday—DeVaughn OOXOO." Particular attention should be paid to the Spanish moss hanging in the trees. For some of the officers and enlisted men of the West Virginia National Guard, this was as far south as they had ever been.

Four

Ordered to the Border

This photograph is of Ann Cochran (left), holding the 2nd Regimental colors, and Charlotte Morrison (right) holding the national colors. These two children were daughters of officers in the 2nd West Virginia National Guard. This photographs was taken in 1916 at Camp Kanawha near present-day Kanawha City, which is near Charleston, the capital of West Virginia. When Pres. Woodrow Wilson called for the National Guard to go into the federal service to punish Pancho Villa for his unjustified and murderous actions of attacking Columbus, New Mexico, along the U.S.–Mexican border, the West Virginia National Guard responded and began preparations to head for the border.

These two pictures of Ann Cochran (left) and Charlotte Morrison (right and below) holding puppies at Camp Kanawha are typical of early photographs showing family members and children of the officers. In many instances, the officers of the regiment took their families with them on some of their maneuvers and housed them in specially made family barracks, which resembled neat little cabins. The photographs at Camp Kanawha are more representative of family members coming to say goodbye to their loved ones as they head for points south along the Mexican border and possibly even action with Villa and his murdering band of outlaw marauders.

The men of the 2nd West Virginia National Guard make ready to move out and serve on the border. West Virginia was one of 48 National Guard units ordered into active duty by President Wilson. The guard's main objective was to protect border settlers and provide the regular army with a reserve force if called upon. Gen. John J. Pershing and the regular U.S. Army would undertake a "punitive expedition" into Mexico to apprehend Villa and his bandits, and, if successful, to punish them for their encroachment and destruction of U.S. property. Upon receiving President Wilson's call to mobilize on June 18th, the 1st and 2nd Regiments were ordered to report to Camp Kanawha. From the time of President Wilson's call, it took the entire West Virginia National Guard only five days to assemble at Camp Kanawha.

Officers and men of the 2nd West Virginia National Guard busy themselves at drill and a bit of public relations at Camp Kanawha. News of Villa's vicious attack on Columbus, New Mexico, angered many of the guardsmen. Seventeen Americans had been killed. Seven members of the 13th U.S. Cavalry had been killed, and eight civilians had died, six of which were summarily executed when Villa's men attacked the hotel. Villa's forces also executed a number of Americans he encountered in his march to Columbus. His men had also raped two women in Columbus. These atrocities made headlines all across the country and prompted President Wilson to take immediate action on March 10, 1916. Villa had managed to flaunt the fact that the Carrancista government could do little to control him, at least in northwestern Mexico.

While the guardsmen readied themselves with military maneuvers and physical conditioning for service on the border, they were also held accountable for personal and overall camp inspections. In this photograph, cots, blankets, and bedrolls are laid out for military inspection. Notice the bell-type tents and how they have been readied for inspection.

Members of the 2nd West Virginia National Guard head out in the mess area at Camp Kanawha. The men were responsible for the daily upkeep of their mess kit and tin plate. Mess kits were inspected thoroughly after each daily use and after each washing to insure proper military guidelines on cleanliness were followed.

These two photographs are excellent views of the bivouac area at Camp Kanawha and the military Post Exchange at the camp. It should be further noted that the men in both pictures are posing to have their pictures taken. The Post Exchange was where a soldier could get a bottle of Coca-Cola or a candy bar, not to mention a number of other items such as stationery, soap, toiletries, and reading material, including books, magazines, or newspapers. The Post Exchange provided a tired or homesick soldier with a window to the outside world that made his military existence just a little more pleasurable or comfortable in a world filled with drill and parade.

This photograph, taken at Camp Kanawha, shows several officers of the 2nd West Virginia National Guard giving the camp a thorough inspection. Such inspections were routine as the guard was expected to function much like the regular U.S. Army in all aspects of military training. At Camp Kanawha, there was no rest for the weary. Soldiers were expected to not only do their designated duties and participate in daily camp drill, but also keep their uniforms clean and in a presentable condition. These young guardsmen are working on keeping their military breeches clean by scrubbing them vigorously with a bar of soap and a stiff bristle brush and then having a friend spray them off with the water spigot stationed close to the cleaning station.

These two photographs feature the stable detail at Camp Kanawha. To alleviate boredom and dissatisfaction in the camp, the men kept busy with drill and a two-day field march from Camp Kanawha to Spring Hill, Kanawha County, several miles to the west. The march was a successful venture that gave the troops a good experience in forced marches and field bivouac techniques. A planned 40-mile march from Camp Kanawha to Clendenin, to begin on August 8th, was cancelled because the War Department would not authorize the regiment to rent horses for the officers to ride. Photographic evidence shows that the officers of the regiment did have fully equipped and serviceable mounts during this time period, but it is not clearly understood why such a request was made by the guard or, for that matter, was denied by the War Department.

These two photographs give an excellent glance into a rare, casual moment during the inspection process. Members of the regimental band stand in various poses of relaxed posture. The men who served in the regimental band had to perform the same daily duties as the other men in the unit, as well as learning and playing music for martial drill and parade. The band played an important part in the esprit de corps of the regiment. In many ways, the band had its roots in the past. Since Colonial times, there was always someone who could play a fife or a drum for the militia units that dotted the state. During the Civil War, West Virginia regimental bands were not uncommon to see. The 2nd Regiment's band was a great source of pride for the men and officers of the unit.

The men of the West Virginia National Guard wait for inspection of their beds and camp gear at Camp Kanawha in Kanawha County, West Virginia. From this photograph, it is apparent that not all of the men are in military dress. A possible explanation for this could be that some of the men were new recruits or lived in Charleston and came as they were after their civilian jobs.

In this 1916 photograph, the men and officers of the West Virginia National Guard are on parade at Camp Kanawha near Charleston, West Virginia. Here an officer reports to the commanding officer while the men of the unit stand at attention and chief musician Harvey L. Gregory waits for his cue to begin the regimental band playing some martial march or patriotic tune.

In these two photographs, the officers of the 2nd West Virginia National Guard come forward to receive their orders from the commanding officer, who is mounted. The other men who are mounted are members of the staff or captains of the various companies who were also mounted in order to better coordinate company maneuvers. According to period records, the men of the West Virginia National Guard were a well-drilled and well-trained unit. The overall regiment also boasted of having some of the best marksmen in the entire National Guard organization all across the United States.

The above photograph is similar to the two previous photographs of the officers of the 2nd West Virginia National Guard receiving their marching orders from their commanding officer. In the photograph below, an officer inspects the men of the regiment to ensure they are following proper military training. The order given was probably "Shoulder Arms!" Drill was a time for seasoned guardsmen to keep their skills sharp and honed, while it was a place for younger men to be directed in the school of the soldier. Poor or dudish behavior in the ranks was not tolerated, and such behavior was quickly dealt with. The men of the unit may have only been guardsmen, but they also had the same training and followed the same rules that governed the regular U.S. Army.

These photographs show guardsmen standing in formation. On August 9, 1916, a severe thunderstorm caused Cabin Creek to overflow its banks, causing a 20-mile path of death and destruction along the narrow hollow, uprooting trees, destroying buildings and railroad tracks, and literally tearing homes from their foundations. On August 10th, news reached Camp Kanawha that a flood had devastated the Cabin Creek area. The 1st Battalion of the 2nd Regiment was immediately mobilized and sent to the area to begin relief efforts. The guard members were then loaded aboard trains with as many emergency travel rations as possible. The trains transported the men as far up Cabin Creek as they could, and the troops carried the rations on foot to the disaster victims who were beyond the reach of the railroad. By late August, the guardsmen had reported back to camp.

This photograph, taken at Camp Kanawha, shows the men of the West Virginia National Guard standing at attention during company formation and drill. It should be noted that all of the enlisted men are dressed in their full day gear and are standing at attention with their 1903 Springfield rifles while an officer looks on.

This photograph pictures the noncommissioned officers of Company E, 2nd West Virginia National Guard. From left to right are (seated) Corporal Shriner, Corporal Renforth, Corporal Smith, Corporal Stephens, and Corporal Moorehead; (standing) First Sergeant Webb, Sergeant Sayer, Sergeant Riley, Sergeant Walton, Sergeant Clovis, Sergeant Shriner, Corp. J. Holland, Corp. D. Holland, and Sergeant Stanley. This photograph was taken at Camp Kanawha in 1916.

In this photograph, Lt. Fred Cochran's battered and worn military-issued hat is amusingly showcased for the men and officers at Camp Kanawha. Cochran even has the dashing flair to model his fine chapeau for his fellow guardsman, as his fellow officer Lt. Charles F. Templeton looks somewhat amused over the whole affair. The men in the unit jokingly called Lieutenant Cochran's fine headgear the "Horrible Hat."

State adjutant general John C. Bond held the rank of brigadier general in the Executive Department of the state while serving as adjutant general of West Virginia. Bond also held the rank of major as a member of the Staff Corps. As state adjutant, Bond reported directly to governor and commander in chief Henry D. Hatfield at the state capitol in Charleston, West Virginia.

Lt. Everett F. Brooks, quartermaster and commissary for the 3rd Battalion, of Charleston, West Virginia, was, according to Lt. Fred Cochran of Company E, known by the alias "Theda B." Brooks is holding the camp cat that the men and officers of Camp Kanawha had made a regimental pet out of.

Lt. Charles F. Templeton of Company E, 2nd West Virginia National Guard, was a native of Huntington, West Virginia. He is seen here petting the camp cat.

Capt. Walter W. White of Company E, 2nd West Virginia National Guard, looks up from his busy schedule of finishing military paperwork on his typewriter at Camp Kanawha. White was a native of Parkersburg, West Virginia.

Maj. Lester Ridenour of the 1st Battalion, 2nd West Virginia National Guard, was from Ward, West Virginia. This photograph was taken at Camp Kanawha in 1916.

Maj. Charles R. Morgan (left) and Lt. Howard E. DeVaughn (right) are standing at Major Morgan's tent at Camp Kanawha. Major Morgan was the state's paymaster and dispensing officer. He was from Charleston, West Virginia, while DeVaughn was from Parkersburg, West Virginia.

Capt. Charles Bell was the head of the 2nd West Virginia National Guard supply company. Bell was from Parkersburg, West Virginia. The supply wagons being pulled by the mules can be seen in this scene at Camp Kanawha in 1916.

Col. Charles E. Morrison is seen here standing abreast of the 2nd Regiment flag and the national colors. Morrison was the commanding officer of the 2nd West Virginia National Guard. He was from Parkersburg, West Virginia. This photograph was taken at Camp Kanawha in 1916 just before the unit set out for duty on the Mexican border.

Lt. Col. John H. Charnock of the 2nd West Virginia National Guard was from Wellsburg, West Virginia. This photograph was taken at Camp Kanawha in 1916. Charnock was second in command of the regiment.

Maj. William Wallace was the U.S. Army mustering in officer who officially mustered the 2nd West Virginia National Guard into the federal service for duty on the American border after President Wilson called for the activation of all National Guard units to be federalized on June 18, 1916. The 2nd Regiment would serve in this capacity until it was mustered out on March 24, 1917.

Lt. Howard E. DeVaughn of the 2nd West Virginia National Guard is pictured at Camp Kanawha near Kanawha City, West Virginia, in 1916.

Lt. Fred Cochran of the 2nd West Virginia National Guard is seen at Camp Kanawha near Kanawha City in 1916.

This photograph is of Col. Charles E. Morrison at Camp Kanawha near Kanawha City, West Virginia, just before heading for duty on the Mexican border in 1916.

From left to right, Lt. Fred M. Cochran, a man believed to be Capt. Charles S. Jackson, and Capt. Walter W. White are all at Camp Kanawha in 1916. All of these men were Parkersburg, West Virginia, residents.

Capt. Antoine August Michel Gaujot was a part of Company F, 2nd West Virginia National Guard. Gaujot had served with Company M, 27th U.S. Volunteers, and was awarded the Medal of Honor for his actions on December 19, 1899, at the Battle of Paye near San Mateo during the Philippine Insurrection. He was officially issued the medal by certified mail on February 15, 1911.

Lt. Fred Cochran takes a moment out of his busy day to rest in his tent. Cochran is seated on his military cot at Camp Kanawha in 1916.

Lieutenant Cochran is seated at the officer's headquarters fly at Camp Kanawha in 1916.

Capt. Walter W. White of Company E, 2nd West Virginia National Guard, is seated at a table while typing. It appears Captain White is still trying to catch up on his schedule of finishing vital military paperwork at Camp Kanawha. White was a native of Parkersburg, West Virginia.

Lt. Fred Cochran (center) is pictured above with other officers of the West Virginia National Guard at a memorial cannon to honor past West Virginia soldiers. It is believed this picture was taken during an outing away from Camp Kanawha and someplace in the vicinity of Kanawha City or Charleston, West Virginia. Note that one of the officers has brought his child, who sits astride the cannon barrel while the family dog is featured standing in the throat of the gun at the front of the muzzle. The photograph below is of one of the officers of the 2nd West Virginia National Guard caught snoozing in the back of Lieutenant Cochran's automobile. The original caption on the back of the photograph states, "Lieutenant Bratt."

Lt. Fred Cochran leads Company E, 2nd West Virginia National Guard, on marching exercises at Camp Kanawha in 1916.

In this 1916 photograph of the parade field at Camp Kanawha, officers are drilling the new recruits of the 2nd West Virginia National Guard. The original caption states, "Drilling the Rookies."

New recruits at Camp Kanawha demonstrate their newfound ability in the "School of the Soldier." These men are executing the Extended Order Drill. This is just the beginning of their formal military training exercises. By the time these young recruits finished up their tour of duty on the border, they had become quite proficient in drill and maneuver tactics.

This photograph in many ways typifies the age-old joke of kitchen patrol duty. In this photograph, taken at Camp Kanawha, members of the West Virginia National Guard peel potatoes for the evening dinner.

This photograph is entitled "Last Meal—Kanawha—W.Va." It appears that the last meal for Company E, 2nd West Virginia National Guard, consisted of mashed potatoes, sliced ham, and bread. It should be noted that some of the young men are grimacing and hamming it up, so to speak, while trying to eat their ham. Others hold the ham bones in their hands and look less than enthusiastic about their last meal at Camp Kanawha, proving the age-old adage that a soldier will always complain about what his dear old Uncle Sam feeds him.

In this photograph at Camp Kanawha, the members of the 2nd West Virginia National Guard gather around to receive orders and instructions concerning their pending movement to the U.S.–Mexican border.

This photograph is titled "Packing up and cleaning up the camp." When the guard left Camp Kanawha, they policed the camp for trash and garbage, as well as misplaced equipment and damaged military equipment that needed to be disposed of or destroyed. The smoke from the fire in the background gives witness to this fact.

This photograph at Camp Kanawha is entitled "The Bedding Roll." Several members of the 2nd West Virginia National Guard work on rolling their bed rolls while an officer and a civilian visitor look on.

This photograph at Camp Kanawha is entitled "Packing up." This is another typical camp scene as the men and officers prepare to pack up their personal and military gear to head for duty on the Mexican border.

An unidentified officer of the West Virginia National Guard on horseback takes one last look at Camp Kanawha before departing for duty on the Mexican border in 1916.

Members of the 2nd West Virginia National Guard are seen here marching out of camp to assemble on the parade ground for closing ceremonies at the camp. Notice the civilians scattered throughout the camp in this picture. Friends, loved ones, and well-wishers all assembled at Camp Kanawha to wish the men of the regiment good-bye and safe journeys.

Spectators gathered at Camp Kanawha near Kanawha City, West Virginia, to wish the departing West Virginia National Guard members good-bye as they prepare to head off for service on the Mexican border in 1916.

These photographs were taken as the members of the 2nd West Virginia National Guard prepared to leave Kanawha County on their last day in camp and just before heading out for the border. The regimental band can be seen in the distance on the left-hand side of these photographs. Members of the 2nd West Virginia National Guard are on parade and preparing to march out of Camp Kanawha.

Members of the 2nd West Virginia National Guard band march by (above) in review before the crowd of well-wishers at Camp Kanawha. The band played a number of patriotic tunes before they took the position of honor and led the regiment to the train, where the guardsmen embarked for points south on the Mexican border. In the photograph below, the men take one last look at home before they head south. It was reported that several of the men in the regiment became homesick during the months of July and August and left the troop, being absent without leave, but fortunately returned before they could be considered deserters. If they had not returned within the 10 days' limit prescribed by military law, it could have resulted in a court-martial and a two-year sentence of hard labor at Fort Leavenworth, Kansas.

After a somewhat lengthy program filled with speeches and good-byes, the men of the 2nd West Virginia National Guard start their march out of Camp Kanawha for the last time and prepare for federal duty on the Mexican border. The mounted officers of the regiment and the members of the Supply Company stand quietly alongside pack horses and mules of the Supply Company while final ceremonies at Camp Kanawha officially come to a close.

The photograph at right of the 2nd West Virginia National Guard is entitled "The Road to the Train." On October 17 and 18, 1916, the regiment broke camp and boarded trains headed for Texas and border duty. The regiment reached Camp Wilson, San Antonio, Texas, on October 12, 1916, and was assigned to the 1st Brigade, 12th Division. The West Virginia National Guard, like the other guard units stationed on the border, was not sent to Mexico along with General Pershing's expeditionary forces but was ordered to protect American civilians and settlements along the border.

This photograph of boats and ships on the Tennessee River was taken by Fred Cochran while the 2nd West Virginia National Guard was traveling by train to start duty along the Mexican border in 1916. It should be noted that the scale of several of the larger ships cannot be determined until comparing them with the sternwheeler in the left-hand corner of this photograph.

As the 2nd West Virginia National Guard members made their way to the border, they stopped by an important Civil War battlefield site. This photograph was taken on top of Lookout Mountain in Chattanooga, Tennessee. This is a Confederate gun position in what is today known as the Point Park Unit of Chickamauga–Chattanooga National Military Park. The gun position is that of Garrity's Alabama Battery.

This 1916 photograph features the officers of the 2nd West Virginia National Guard posing in front of the New York monument at Lookout Mountain in Chattanooga, Tennessee.

This is an unidentified Civil War monument. The location of this monument is also unidentified. It has been speculated that this monument may be in the Shiloh, Chickamauga, or Chattanooga area, but at the present time, it cannot be identified by National Park Service officials.

In this photograph, entitled "Headquarters Ordered to the Border," Fred Cochran deliberately took the last picture of the headquarters tent at Camp Kanawha and contrasted it with the next photograph of the headquarters tent at Camp Wilson, San Antonio, Texas. The contrast of the camp geography between the two locations is apparent in these photographs.

Col. C. E. Morrison poses for this photograph in front of the 2nd West Virginia National Guard headquarters tent at Camp Wilson in San Antonio, Texas. Morrison and the other commanding officers of the state guard units almost immediately began their border service duty upon arriving at Camp Wilson.

In these two photographs, Fred Cochran and the other officers of the 2nd West Virginia National Guard take some time out of their busy schedules to go sightseeing around the countryside and visit a few of the Spanish missions that dot the vicinity around San Antonio, Texas. Photographic evidence proves that the officers of the 2nd West Virginia National Guard made several outings to sightsee during their seven-month stay while serving on the Mexican border.

Here in San Antonio, the quiet, calm, cool waters of the San Antonio River are showcased as the river winds its way through the town.

In this image, taken near San Antonio, buzzards and burros are featured. The title of this photograph is "BUZZARDS—TEXAS."

Photographer F. L. Lamphere features the home of a poor Mexican family near San Antonio, Texas. Sites such as this were not uncommon during this time period.

In this photograph, an unidentified officer of the 2nd West Virginia National Guard is seated at one of the Mexican homes on the American side of the Rio Grande River. The land in the distance and across the river is Mexico.

Upon their arrival at Camp Wilson, the members of the 2nd West Virginia National Guard took part in several parades for the people of San Antonio. In this photograph, a float has been decorated with the patriotic theme of George Washington and his troops at Valley Forge.

This image of the parade at San Antonio, Texas, in 1916 features the ladies of the American Red Cross along with a woman dressed in an American flag, symbolizing the figure of the republic, "Columbia."

These members of the National Guard ride in a float that is a representation of a fortified bastion of American strength. Notice the guardsmen with the 1903 Springfield rifles and the cannon barrel protruding from the tower turret.

In this photograph of the 1916 San Antonio parade, Spanish-type equestrian riders are seen patiently standing in front of Reed's Drug Store.

In the 1916 San Antonio parade, a float has been designed to represent a Greek or Roman style of architecture. It would appear that the float represents the Aesop's Fable of Androcles and the Lion.

In this photograph of the 1916 San Antonio parade, it would appear that Little Bo Peep has found her sheep and she is taking them home while she can. It is uncertain why some of the floats took on a whimsical theme.

Members of the 2nd West Virginia National Guard work their way down the streets of San Antonio in the 1916 San Antonio parade with a heavy artillery gun in tow while spectators look on.

Here, in the 1916 San Antonio parade, members of the National Guard pass the city bank as they wheel their artillery piece around the corner.

In this photograph of the 1916 San Antonio parade, members of the National Guard march past spectators in the streets of San Antonio, Texas.

Here members of the National Guard pass the Drogueria del Refugio in the 1916 San Antonio parade.

In this photograph, Lt. Col. John H. Charnock, who is pictured here standing in the corner of some ruins beside his Mexican guide, toured the area around San Antonio, Texas, with other officers of the 2nd West Virginia National Guard while at Camp Wilson.

This is a 1916 view of the Rio Grande River looking across to the Mexican side of the border.

This picturesque view of one of the towns along the Rio Grande River was taken in 1916 by Lt. Fred Cochran of the 2nd West Virginia National Guard.

This is a picture of a small, unidentified building, probably a home, taken by Lt. Fred Cochran of the 2nd West Virginia National Guard while on an outing in 1916 near San Antonio, Texas.

Lt. Fred Cochran of the 2nd West Virginia National Guard took this photograph near San Antonio, Texas, in 1916. He writes the following description on the back of the photograph: "This will give you some idea of Broadway Squawtown."

In this image, Lt. Fred Cochran of the 2nd West Virginia National Guard (far right) confers with a member of the clergy. The other individuals in this photograph are unidentified.

This is a panoramic view of Fort Sam Houston taken in 1916.

In this photograph by F. L. Lamphere, bayonet combat at Fort Sam Houston is being practiced. Note the heavy padding, fencing masks, and the blunted, pigtail practice bayonets the men are using.

This is an armored motor car at Fort Sam Houston, Texas. This photograph was taken in 1916.

In this photograph, taken at Fort Sam Houston in 1916, members of the regular U.S. Army and the West Virginia National Guard are shown practicing their machine gun skills. Note the two spotters with binoculars calling out target accuracy. The caption on this photograph reads, "School of Musketry, Machine Gun target practice Fort Sam Houston, Texas." Fred Cochran titles this photograph "The Colt Machine Gun."

F. L. Lamphere took this image of members of the 7th Machine Gun Troop firing the Lewis machine gun. The sergeant holding the spare ammunition canister is wearing a canteen with crossed rifles. Above the crossed rifles is the number 7, and below the rifles are the initials M. G., meaning machine gun. This is probably a photograph of regular U.S. Army troops.

This photograph was originally titled "In the Pit." Lt. Fred Cochran titles this photograph "In the Pit at Leon Springs, Texas." Leon Springs was the target range used by the regular U.S. Army and was also utilized by the various National Guard units that came south to do border duty.

In this photograph, members of Company E, 2nd West Virginia National Guard, proudly display their trophy award for outstanding marksmanship won at Camp Wilson, Texas. The men in Company E were known as crack shots. Several of the men had previously gone to national

competitions against other guardsmen from all across the country and made a good showing of what real West Virginia sharpshooting was all about.

In this rare photograph, Lt. Fred Cochran and other officers of the 2nd West Virginia National Guard pose with an early airplane at the Stenson School of Aviation. From left to right are Lieutenant Riley, Captain White, Lieutenant Cochran, Captain Holswade, Lieutenant Lakin, and the pilot.

Here Lt. Fred Cochran of the 2nd West Virginia National Guard poses outside of his tent at Camp Wilson, Texas.

This photograph is listed as "The General Court—Camp Wilson, Texas." The men are identified from left to right as follows: Captain Harper of the 1st Mississippi; Lieutenant Cochran of the 2nd West Virginia; Captain Holswade of the 2nd West Virginia; Lieutenant Blout of the 1st Mississippi; Major Ridenour of the 2nd West Virginia; Captain Nolan of the 7th Illinois; Major Dallsey of the 1st Mississippi; Captain Ford of the 2nd West Virginia, Judge Advocate; Captain Bartlett of the 1st Mississippi; unidentified lieutenant of the 7th Illinois; unidentified court reporter; Lieutenant Chapman of the 2nd West Virginia; and Captain Smith of the 7th Texas Council.

Pictured here is Capt. Harry Holswade of Company D, 2nd West Virginia National Guard, at Camp Wilson, Texas.

This photograph is of Lieutenant Curry (left) and Capt. Antoine Gaujot of Company F. Like Gaujot, his brother, Julien E. Gaujot, also won a Medal of Honor on April 13, 1911, for rescuing 5 American citizens and 25 Mexican soldiers from bandits on the Mexican border. When he was first told about Antoine's medal, Julien said, "I got to get me one of them things for myself if I bust."

Pictured is Capt. Antoine Gaujot of Company F, 2nd West Virginia National Guard. Only eight pairs of brothers have won the Medal of Honor. Gaujot and his brother, Julien, won theirs in two different campaigns. Julien Gaujot was the only soldier in American history to win his medal for actions of a peacekeeping nature. Capt. Antoine August Michel Gaujot is buried at the Fairview Cemetery in Williamson, West Virginia.

Near San Antonio, Texas, in 1916 are, from left to right, Lieutenant Lakin, Capt. Harry Holswade, Lieutenant Riley, Lt. Fred Cochran, and Captain White.

This 1916 photograph appears to be out of place in the Cochran Collection, as it is probably from Camp Kanawha. The subject in question is adjutant general John C. Bond of the 2nd West Virginia National Guard.

Lt. Fred Cochran of the 2nd West Virginia National Guard is pictured here standing outside of his tent at Camp Wilson, Texas.

In this 1916 photograph, taken at Camp Wilson, Texas, an officer of the 2nd West Virginia National Guard holds up the colors for the cameraman.

In this 1916 view of the Alamo Plaza, San Antonio, Texas, the whole plaza is filled with a multitude of activity. The back of the Alamo can be seen on the left side of the photograph.

In 1916, this soldier at the entrance of the Alamo prepares to call to officers on horseback as they pass while other enlisted men and civilians prepare to cross the street.

Above is an image of Mission San Jose taken in 1916. The mission was founded in 1720 and was rebuilt in 1768 and 1782. It is the largest of the five missions in San Antonio and is known as the "Queen Mission." This Spanish frontier mission served the Coahuitecan Indian population, instructing them in the Catholic religion and teaching European beliefs. The site was an important military outpost in the early days of the mission but proved to become more important in the purpose of saving souls and aiding the indigenous population. In the photograph below, officers of the 2nd West Virginia National Guard are seen at the mission. From left to right are Lieutenant Riley, Lieutenant Lakin, Captain White, Captain Holswade, and Lieutenant Cochran.

In this photograph, taken at Mission San Jose, Texas, in 1916, the members of the 2nd West Virginia National Guard pose on the outer edge of the roof of the mission. From front to back are Lieutenant Casper, Lieutenant Scott, Lieutenant Johnson, Lieutenant Northcoat, Captain White, Lieutenant Lakin, Captain Holswade, Lieutenant Riley, and Lieutenant Brooks.

This is another photograph of the officers of the West Virginia National Guard at what is believed to be Mission San Jose, Texas. The image did not have any documentation but was with the Mission San Jose section of the Fred Cochran Collection.

Here the officers of the 2nd West Virginia stand in front of Mission San Jose. From left to right are Captain White, Lieutenant Brooks, Lieutenant Scott, Lieutenant Johnson, Lieutenant Lakin, Lieutenant Cochran, Lieutenant Riley, Lieutenant Northcoat, Lieutenant Casper, Captain Bell, and Captain Holswade.

The Mission San Jose near San Antonio, Texas, is constructed of limestone and has two domes and one tower. It has elaborate baroque-faced stone carving and an intricately carved rose window. The date of construction in this photograph is in error. The mission was founded in 1720, and the present mission was constructed in 1768 and 1782, according to the U.S. National Park Service.

It would appear that the men of the 2nd West Virginia National Guard also visited the Mission Conception while in San Antonio, Texas. The date of construction in this photograph is in error. According to the U.S. National Park Service, the mission was established in 1731, and the present mission was constructed from 1740 to 1755.

This photograph of the Mission Conception near San Antonio, Texas, was taken in 1916 while members of the 2nd West Virginia National Guard were doing duty on the Mexican border.

The next seven photographs in the Fred Cochran Collection are unidentified but are believed to be the officers of the 2nd West Virginia National Guard in civilian clothing meeting an official or person of note someplace near San Antonio, Texas, in 1916. The exact location is unidentified.

These photographs in the Fred Cochran Collection are unidentified but are believed to be the officers of the 2nd West Virginia National Guard in civilian clothing meeting an official or person of note someplace near San Antonio, Texas in 1916. The exact location is unidentified.

In these two pictures, members of the 2nd West Virginia National Guard are meeting with an official or important person near San Antonio. Note the official greeting committee is composed of the unidentified official and two other men, who are obviously singing and playing a guitar as a gesture of greeting to the officers of the West Virginia National Guard.

Here members of the 2nd West Virginia National Guard have been given gifts of flowers and alcohol after a meeting somewhere near San Antonio, Texas.

In this photograph by F. J. Lamphere, a Mexican family poses in front of their home along the Mexican border. Small Mexican farms like this one dotted the banks of the Rio Grande around 1916.

F. J. Lamphere took this image of members of the regular U.S. Army as they lie prone, ready to fire upon the order of the commanding officer. This photograph was probably taken near Fort Wilson or Fort Sam Houston, Texas.

In this photograph by F. J. Lamphere, the "Three Inch Gun" that was used against Pancho Villa and his bandits is featured. This gun was hauled by a team of horses across the Mexican border and brought into action several times during General Pershing's Punitive Expedition.

In this F. J. Lamphere photograph, the mounted artillery that was used in General Pershing's Punitive Expedition against Pancho Villa is shown en route to Mexico. The guns and their ammunition caissons can be clearly seen here.

Fred J. Lamphere took this photograph of the 4.7 Siege gun firing a 60-pound projectile while in action somewhere near Mexico. According to the writing on the photograph, the gun had a maximum range of 11,000 yards.

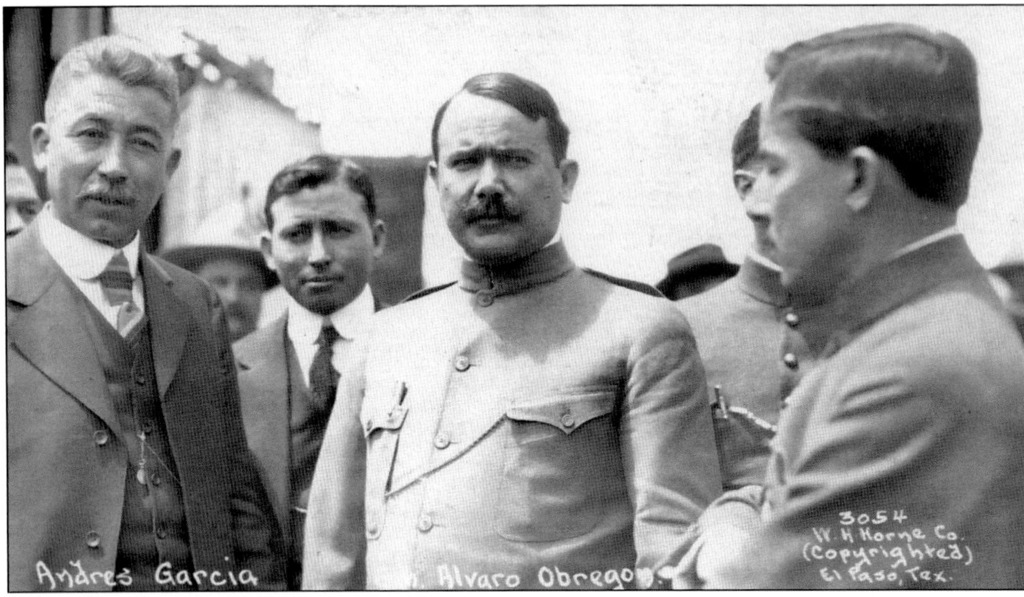

This is a photographic postcard by W. H. Horne Company of El Paso, Texas, featuring officials of the Mexican government. This image was probably taken when members of the 10th U.S. Cavalry were released to American officials after a skirmish with regular Mexican forces at the battle of Carrizal, Mexico. Here are Andres Garcia (left), Mexican consul in El Paso, Texas, and Mexican general Alvaro Obregon (right).

This photographic postcard, printed by W. H. Horne Company of El Paso, features members of the 10th U.S. Cavalry, who were released to American officials after a skirmish on June 21, 1916, with Mexican federal forces at the battle of Carrizal, Mexico. In this action, 2 American officers and 4 enlisted men were killed and 23 were taken prisoner. Gen. Felix Gomez and 45 Mexican soldiers also died.

In this 1916 photograph, it appears the man in the air is either jumping or climbing over a barbed-wire fence for a training exercise demonstration. This image is believed to have been taken at Camp Wilson, Texas.

This picture in the Fred Cochran Collection is not identified, but it is believed to be of the 2nd West Virginia National Guard band playing for the soldiers and spectators at Camp Wilson or Fort Sam Houston, Texas. After nearly seven months of service with the 12th Division, the West Virginia National Guard was ordered to Huntington, West Virginia, to be mustered out of federal service on March 24, 1917.

In April 1917, President Wilson called the guard for military duty in Europe. The 1st and 2nd Regiments were mobilized, and by April 10th, both units were mustered into the federal service. The regiments were ordered to protect vital lines of transportation and industry in the state that might be prone to espionage or attempted sabotage. Ann and Fred Cochran (in the car) are pictured here with another officer of the 2nd West Virginia.

Ann Cochran is seen here playing near Camp Shelby, Mississippi. Nearly the entire West Virginia National Guard responded to Wilson's call of April 1917. In September 1917, the 1st and 2nd Regiments reported to Camp Shelby, Mississippi. The 2nd was incorporated into the 38th Infantry Division, comprised of National Guard units from West Virginia, Virginia, Indiana, and Kentucky. The organization was later redesignated as the 150th Infantry Regiment.

Ann Cochran is seen here playing near Camp Shelby, Mississippi. When the 1st West Virginia National Guard reached Camp Shelby, it was broken up to fill other units. The regiment was reorganized into the 113th Engineer Train, 137th Machine Gun Battalion, 113th Engineers, and the 113th Ammunition Train, all part of the 38th Division. While at Camp Shelby, the West Virginians underwent nearly a year of training and garrison duty.

Ann Cochran is seen here playing near Camp Shelby, Mississippi.

Ann Cochran and an unidentified boy, who was probably a child of one of the other officers of the 2nd West Virginia National Guard, are seen standing in front of one of the officer's family cabins at Camp Shelby, Mississippi, in 1917.

In this photograph, an unidentified enlisted man, an officer, and a small boy are seen working in the woodpile near one of the officer's family cabins at Camp Shelby, Mississippi, in 1917. The inscription on the back of this photograph reads, "Peel head pole—Arthur."

In 1917, the officers and men of the 2nd West Virginia National Guard are in the process of learning the maneuvers for hauling and firing a field artillery piece at Camp Shelby, Mississippi. Here several field artillery drivers are practicing with two pairs of artillery horses.

In this 1917 photograph, taken at Camp Shelby, Mississippi, the men of the 2nd West Virginia National Guard are in the process of learning the maneuvers for the teams of horses used for hauling the field artillery. It is believed that they are working with a 3-inch gun in this photograph.

This 1917 photograph, taken at Camp Shelby, Mississippi, shows the officers of the 2nd West Virginia National Guard conferring with an unidentified officer of the regular U.S. Army on the operation procedures being implemented in the training maneuver of the field artillery. It is believed that a 3-inch gun is pictured here.

In this 1917 image from the Fred Cochran Collection, two unidentified officers and a small girl are chopping and sawing scrap wood for the cooking and heating stoves used at the officer's family quarters at Camp Shelby, Mississippi.

Here in 1917, two small boys and the wife of one of the West Virginia National Guard officers is posed in front of one of the military housing units set aside for the officers and their families at Camp Shelby, Mississippi. It was not uncommon for the officers of a regiment to be allowed to have their families on or near the military reserves of this time period.

In this 1917 photograph from the Fred Cochran Collection, an unidentified officer of the 2nd West Virginia National Guard is seen here along with the children of the other officers of the regiment in the never-ending task of chopping and collecting wood for heating and cooking at Camp Shelby.

Charlotte Morrison (far left) and Ann Cochran (far right) are pictured in 1917 with an unidentified officer of the 2nd West Virginia National Guard, who is out gathering wood on a wood detail at Camp Shelby, Mississippi.

In this 1917 photograph, an unidentified officer of the 2nd West Virginia National Guard is gathering wood with three children who are on wood detail at Camp Shelby, Mississippi.

In 1917, the children of the regiment take a well-needed rest from gathering wood while an unidentified officer of the 2nd West Virginia National Guard looks for wood to chop in the background.

Here at Camp Shelby, Mississippi, in 1917, Ann Cochran is playing on a swing with an unidentified boy, who was the child of one of the other officers of the 2nd West Virginia National Guard.

In this 1917 photograph, Charlotte Morrison and Ann Cochran help an unidentified officer of the 2nd West Virginia National Guard look for dead tree branches that can be pulled down.

In this 1917 photograph, an unidentified officer of the 2nd West Virginia National Guard looks for dead tree branches that are suitable to be cut up and used for firewood at the officer's family cabins located at Camp Shelby, Mississippi.

Charlotte Morrison (left) and Ann Cochran (right) are seated in 1917 on a large tree stump near the area of the officer's family quarters at Camp Shelby, Mississippi.

In this 1917 photograph, taken at Camp Shelby, Mississippi, the children of the officers of the 2nd West Virginia National Guard pose as they play and help in the chore of gathering firewood for the cooking and heating stoves placed in each cabin.

In these two 1917 photographs, the cabins of the 2nd West Virginia National Guard officers and their families are featured. In many respects, the military housing units were efficient and in some ways resemble modern-day getaway homes or camping and hunting cabins.

This is another view of one of the military housing units used by the officers of the West Virginia National Guard and their families while stationed at Camp Shelby, Mississippi, in 1917.

The mounted officers of the 38th Division are making an inspection of the various state regiments of the National Guard that made up the 38th Division in 1918. Drilling, training exercises, and division maneuvers were practiced on the immense drill field and parade grounds, which encircled the main headquarters building at Camp Shelby, Mississippi.

In this photograph, taken at Camp Shelby, Mississippi, in 1918, the guardsmen of the 38th Division are on military parade. Notice the reviewing grandstands in the background and the civilians that line the field to wish loved ones good-bye as they prepare to head out for duty in France.

At Camp Shelby, Mississippi, in 1918, the guardsmen of the 38th Division are on military parade. When the 38th Division was redesignated the 150th Infantry Regiment, it was given the nickname "The Old Gray Mare" after the song that was used each morning to wake up the troops.

In this 1918 panoramic photograph, the 38th Division prepares to ship out for service in France. The 38th Division was not sent overseas until October 2, 1918. The 150th Infantry was sent to Chatillon-sur-Seine and then to Le Mans. Shortly after they reached Le Mans, the armistice was signed, and the regiment was quickly rotated back to the states and mustered out in January 1919. The West Virginia guardsmen who were in the various support units for the 38th Division

remained in Europe until March 1919. Upon returning home, the 1st Regiment was fazed out of existence. When the U.S. government released the men from service, it also nullified any prior obligations the members of the regiments owed the state. In effect, the West Virginia National Guard ceased to exist after World War I and was not reestablished until 1921.

The 1872-pattern U.S. belt plate (top) was the standard-issue belt plate used by most of the enlisted men in the West Virginia National Guard during the Spanish-American War period. The eagle-pattern button with arrows in its left talon (center) had been redesigned just prior to the Spanish-American War. Many of the soldiers criticized the unflattering pattern and jokingly called it the turkey button. The 1874 officer's pattern belt plate (bottom) was used during the Indian War and Spanish-American War time periods.

The collar disk on the left belonged to a member of Company B, 1st West Virginia National Guard. The "W.VA" collar disk on the right also belonged to the same man. Company B was from Ritchie County, West Virginia. The button in the center is of the West Virginia state seal. These styles of uniform furniture were used by the members of the West Virginia National Guard from around 1903 until 1918.

Pictured in the top row from left to right are the 1909-pattern Great Seal button, the World War I U.S. collar disk, and the 1909-pattern Great Seal hat disk; pictured below the buttons is a U.S. collar insignia pin. All of these were issued by the U.S. Army and were used by the men and officers of the West Virginia National Guard after they had been federalized for service in World War I.

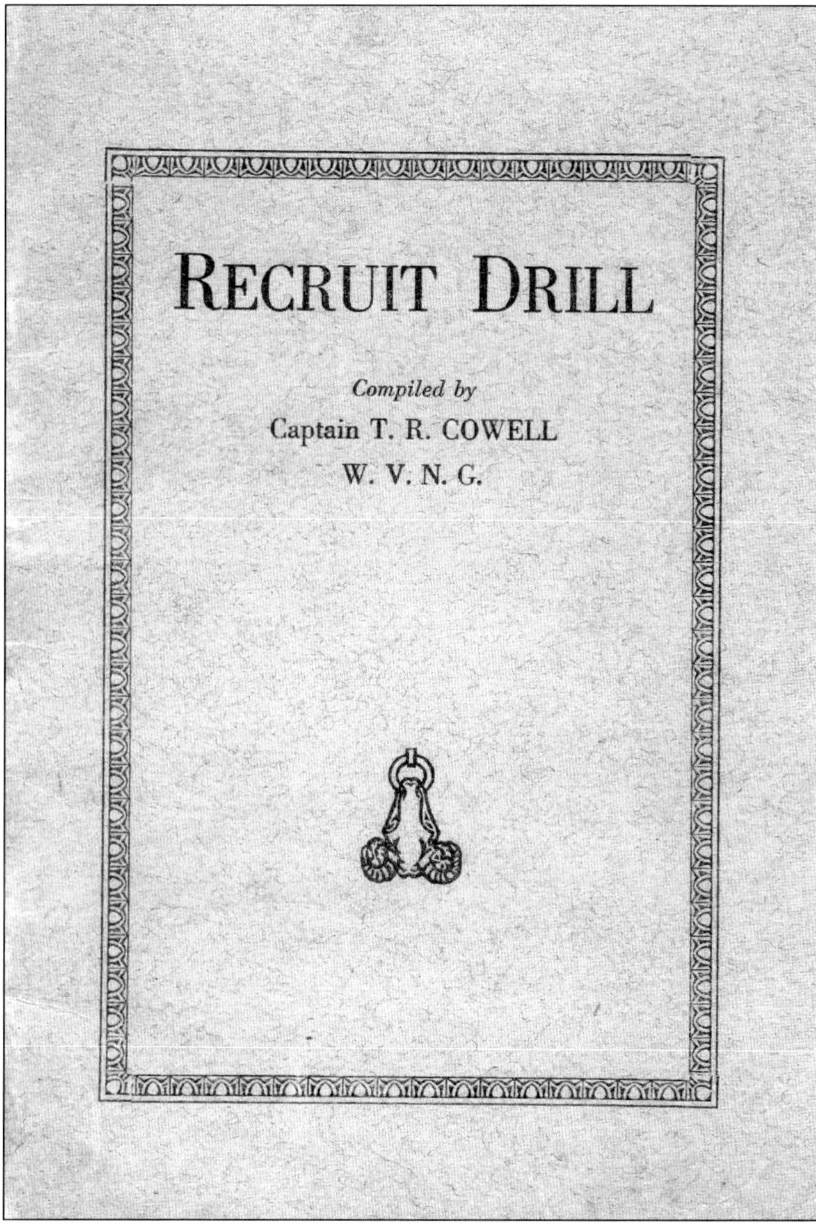

This is a photograph of the "Recruit Drill" manual compiled by Capt. T. Richard Cowell of Parkersburg, West Virginia. The pamphlet is not dated but is believed to be from around 1910. Captain Cowell had been so seriously injured in a train wreck, which occurred at Pleasant View, West Virginia, on May 1, 1907, that physicians on the scene pronounced his injuries as probably fatal. Adjutant general S. B. Baker of Clarksburg was also on the train and was reported as badly shaken up in the wreck but did not require the attention of physicians. Ironically, Captain Cowell recovered from his serious injuries, and several days later, Adjutant Baker died from internal bleeding and injuries he sustained in the wreck. The train was reported as traveling at 60 miles an hour when it left the track 3 miles south of Ravenswood. It was determined that the wreck was caused by a defective rail. Camp Baker at Ravenswood, West Virginia, was later named in memory of Adjutant Baker and was in operation during the 1913 Ohio River flood.

SCHOOL OF THE SOLDIER.

The instructor explains briefly each movement, first executing it himself if practicable. He requires the recruits to take the proper positions unassisted and does not touch them for the purpose of correcting them, except when they are unable to correct themselves. He avoids keeping them too long at the same movement, although each should be understood before passing to another. He exacts by degrees the desired precision and uniformity.

In order that all may advance as rapidly as their abilities permit, the recruits are grouped according to proficiency as instruction progresses. Those who lack aptitude and quickness are separated from the others and placed under experienced drill masters.

INSTRUCTION WITHOUT ARMS.

For preliminary instruction a number of recruits, usually not exceeding three or four, are formed as a squad in single rank.

Position of the Soldier, or Attention.

Heels on the same line and as near each other as the conformation of the man permits.

Feet turned out equally and forming an angle of about 45 degrees.

Knees straight without stiffness.

Hips level and drawn back slightly; body erect and resting equally on hips; chest lifted and arched; shoulders square and falling equally.

Arms and hands hanging naturally, thumb along the seam of the trousers.

Head erect and squarely to the front, chin drawn

—6—

in so the axis of the head and neck is vertical; eyes straight to the front.

Weight of the body resting equally upon the heels and balls of the feet.

The Rests.

Being at a halt, the commands are: **FALL OUT; REST; AT EASE;** and, 1. **Parade,** 2. **Rest.**

At the commond **fall out,** the men may leave the ranks, but are required to remain in the immediate vicinity. They resume their former places, at attention, at the command **fall in.**

At the command **rest** each man keeps one foot in place, but is not required to preserve silence or immobility.

At the command **at ease** each man keeps one foot in place and is required to preserve silence but not immobility.

1. **Parade,** 2. **REST.** Carry the right foot 6 inches straight to the rear, left knee slightly bent; clasp the hands, without constraint, in front of the center of the body, fingers joined, left hand uppermost, left thumb clasped by the thumb and forefinger of the right hand; preserve silence and steadiness of position.

To resume the attention: 1. **Squad,** 2. **ATTENTION.**

The men take the position of the soldier.

Eyes Right or Left.

1. **Eyes,** 2. **RIGHT (LEFT),** 3. **FRONT.**

At the command **right,** turn the head to the right oblique, eqes fixed on the line of eyes of the men in, or supposed to be in, the same rank. At the command **front,** turn the head and eyes to the front.

—7—

Pictured here are pages six and seven of the "Recruit Drill" manual compiled by Capt. T. Richard Cowell of Parkersburg, West Virginia. This section of the manual deals with the "School of the Soldier" and gives instruction in proper drill and evolution of movement. This manual dates from around 1910.

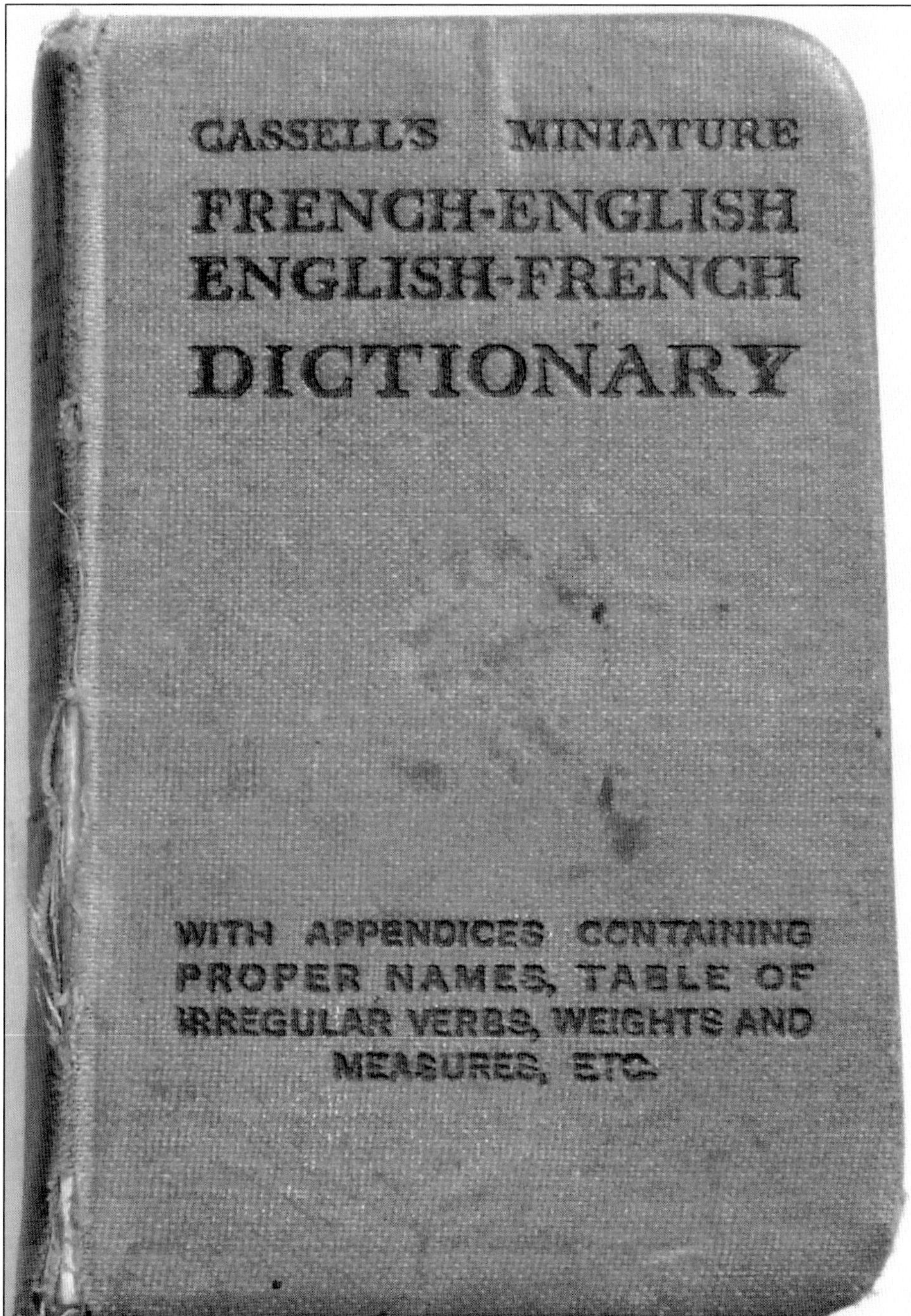

This image is of *Cassell's Miniature French-English, English-French Dictionary* that was used by Landis Stoneking while he was stationed in France. Stoneking, a resident of Lima, West Virginia, was born on August 7, 1891, in Tyler County, West Virginia. He was inducted into military service on June 25, 1918, at Middlebourne, West Virginia. His service records state, "Ser# 3634346; Co. H, 2nd Inf. Repl. & Tng Bn to Aug 12, 1918; 254 Co. 127 Bn. MPC to discharge Pvt. 1/cl—Nov 1, 1918 to July 23, 1919; Honorably disch. July 30, 1919; served overseas—Aug 13, 1918 to July 23, 1919."

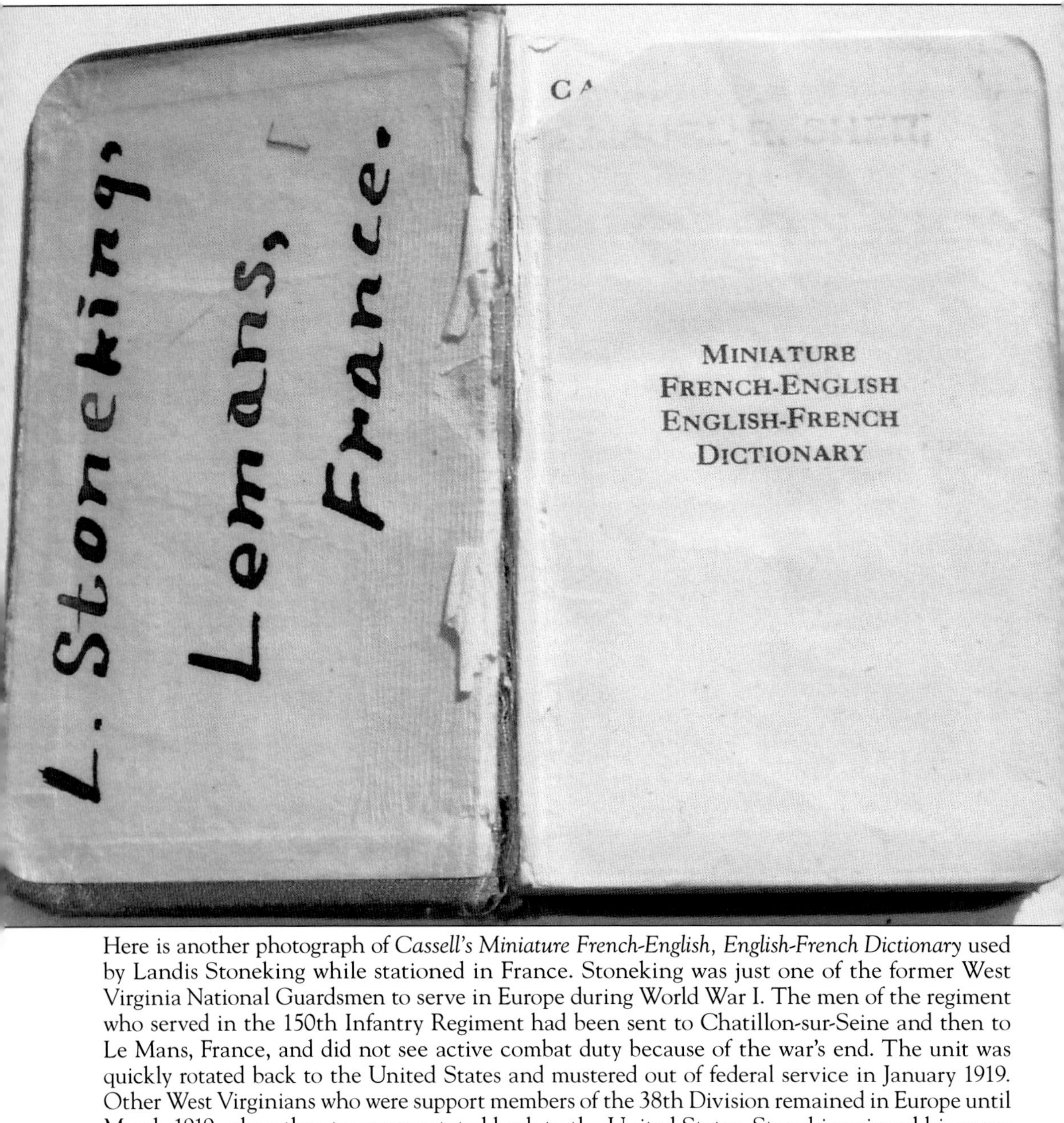

Here is another photograph of *Cassell's Miniature French-English, English-French Dictionary* used by Landis Stoneking while stationed in France. Stoneking was just one of the former West Virginia National Guardsmen to serve in Europe during World War I. The men of the regiment who served in the 150th Infantry Regiment had been sent to Chatillon-sur-Seine and then to Le Mans, France, and did not see active combat duty because of the war's end. The unit was quickly rotated back to the United States and mustered out of federal service in January 1919. Other West Virginians who were support members of the 38th Division remained in Europe until March 1919, when they too were rotated back to the United States. Stoneking signed his name and "LeMans" in this dictionary.

The following 10 images are from the Camp Zachery Taylor Souvenir Folder that was sent home by Osie Morehead to his mother and sister when he and other members of the West Virginia National Guard were doing training exercises there.

Checking Up the New Recruits, Camp Zachary Taylor, Louisville, Ky.

The exact date of the folder is unknown because the time-dated stamp was removed from the folder by some stamp collector many years ago.

Camp Taylor was one of the largest World War I training camps constructed on the North American continent.

The camp consisted of more than 3,000 acres and was constructed in 1917. It was dismantled in 1921.

Today a modern residential area and light commercial area occupy the former military training ground at Louisville, Kentucky.

The neighborhood where the former camp was located is now known as Camp Taylor.

This is the last postcard photograph from the Camp Zachery Taylor Souvenir Folder that was sent home by Osie Morehead. In viewing these photographs, it should be noted that they were originally color tinted with various shades of red, green, blue, brown, and yellow. This process of early colorization did not lend itself to better quality photography. When these photographs were set as black-and-white images for this publication, this fact was made more apparent.

This is a felt pendant from Camp Lee, Virginia, that dates from around 1917. This pendant, at one time, belonged to Landis Stoneking, who was a member of the West Virginia National Guard. Camp Lee was built in 1917 and was dismantled in 1920. The camp had been named in honor of Confederate general Robert E. Lee. The camp was used for enlisted training, replacement, and officer training, and served as a veterinary training camp from 1917 to 1919. More than 134,000 men were trained at Camp Lee during World War I. When the camp was dismantled in 1920, it was turned into a wildlife sanctuary for the Commonwealth of Virginia. With the outbreak of war in Europe in September 1939, the camp was ordered reactivated and rebuilt in November 1940. In the spring of 1950, Camp Lee was renamed Fort Lee.